MAKE YOUR OWN

LAVA LAMP

BY CHRISTOPHER HARBO

PEBBLE
a capstone imprint

Published by Pebble, an imprint of Capstone
1710 Roe Crest Drive, North Mankato, Minnesota 56003
capstonepub.com

Copyright © 2026 by Capstone. All rights reserved. No part of this publication may be reproduced in whole or in part, or stored in a retrieval system, or transmitted in any form or by any means, electronic, mechanical, photocopying, recording, or otherwise, without written permission of the publisher.

Library of Congress Cataloging-in-Publication Data is available on the Library of Congress website.
ISBN: 9798875225192 (hardcover)
ISBN: 9798875225024 (paperback)
ISBN: 9798875225154 (ebook PDF)

Summary: Learn about chemical reactions with this easy and fun science project! Follow the steps and clear photos to make a lava lamp out of household supplies.

Editorial Credits
Editor: Erika L. Shores; Designer: Heidi Thompson; Media Researcher: Jo Miller; Production Specialist: Tori Abraham

Image Credits
Capstone: Karon Dubke: all project photos, supplies; Shutterstock: Ksana Durand, 5, margaryta, 7 (water)

The publisher and the author shall not be liable for any damages allegedly arising from the information in this book, and they specifically disclaim any liability from the use or application of any of the contents of this book.

Any additional websites and resources referenced in this book are not maintained, authorized, or sponsored by Capstone. All product and company names are trademarks™ or registered® trademarks of their respective holders.

Printed and bound in China. 6274

TABLE OF CONTENTS

Lava Lamp Science 4

What You Need 6

What You Do 8

Take It Further 20

Behind the Science 22

Glossary 24

About the Author 24

Words in **BOLD** are in the glossary.

LAVA LAMP SCIENCE

Lava lamps were popular 50 years ago. Inside these lamps, gooey-looking globs of wax rose and fell like flowing lava. Would you like to make your own lava lamp? All it takes is a few supplies and some simple science!

WHAT YOU NEED

- water
- tall glass jar
- vegetable oil
- food coloring
- **effervescent tablet**
- flashlight

WHAT YOU DO

STEP 1

Pour water into the jar until the jar is about one-fourth full.

STEP 2

Pour vegetable oil into the jar until the jar is about three-fourths full.

STEP 3

Let the jar stand until the water and oil separate completely.

Notice how the oil sits on the top of the water.

STEP 4

Drip six to eight drops of food coloring into the jar.

Watch the food coloring fall through the oil and then mix with the water.

15

STEP 5

Break the **effervescent tablet** into three or four pieces.

Turn on the flashlight. Place it behind the jar so light shines through the water.

STEP 6

Drop the effervescent tablet pieces into the jar one at a time.

Watch your lava lamp come to life!

TAKE IT FURTHER

Ask an adult to help you make a snowstorm in a whole new lava lamp. Start by mixing a little white paint into the water. Then use baby oil instead of vegetable oil. Drop in the effervescent tablet pieces to see a **blizzard** begin.

BEHIND THE SCIENCE

Your lava lamp uses differences in **density** and a **chemical reaction** to work. As you saw, vegetable oil does not mix with water and food coloring. The oil floats on top because it is less dense than the water.

Adding the tablet causes a chemical reaction. This reaction releases bubbles of **carbon dioxide** gas. These gas bubbles carry colored water with them as they float up through the oil.

carbon dioxide gas

23

GLOSSARY

blizzard (BLIZ-urd)—a heavy snowstorm with strong wind

carbon dioxide (KAHR-buhn dy-AHK-syd)—a colorless, odorless gas

chemical reaction (KE-muh-kuhl ree-AK-shuhn)—a process in which one or more substances are made into a new substance or substances

density (DEN-si-tee)—a physical property that measures how closely packed together a substance's particles are

effervescent tablet (eff-uhr-VES-uhnt TAB-let)—a tablet that dissolves and forms bubbles when it contacts water

lava (LAH-vuh)—the hot, liquid rock that pours out of a volcano when it erupts

ABOUT THE AUTHOR

Christopher Harbo is a children's book editor from Minnesota who loves reading and writing. During his career, he has helped publish countless fiction and nonfiction books—and has even written a few too. His favorite nonfiction topics include science and history. His favorite fiction books feature superheroes, adventurers, and space aliens.